Round and Round

Written by Alison Hawes

Illustrated by Neil Chapman

"Look at this," said Miss Miller.

"It is going round and round, too!" said Alice.

"Look at this, Dad!" said Alice. "The colours go round and round in the wind!"

"Come and look at this, Alice," said Dad. "We can go tonight!"

Alice went round and round on the helter-skelter.

Then she went round and round on the big wheel.

She went round and round and up and down on the merry-go-round!

"Look at the colours," said Alice. "They are going round and round like me!"

"Did you like the fair?" said Dad.

"Yes," said Alice.

"But now *I* am going…"

round and round and round and round and round and round and round and round